EssaySnark's Strategies for the
2014-'15 MBA Application for
NYU STERN SCHOOL OF BUSINESS

EssaySnark's Strategies for the 2014-'15 MBA Application for NYU STERN SCHOOL OF BUSINESS

by EssaySnark®

Snarkolicious Press

First published October 26, 2011
Latest edition June 8, 2014
version 4.0

Snarkolicious Press
P.O. Box 50021
Palo Alto, CA 94303

www.snarkoliciouspress.com

978 1 938098 23 9

© 2011-2014 by EssaySnark®

Cover image © Eric Isselée, used under license from Fotolia.com

EssaySnark® is a registered trademark. All rights reserved.

No part of this book may be reproduced or transmitted in any form or by any means, electronic or mechanical, including photocopying, recording, transcribing, or by an information storage system, without permission from the publisher. Essay questions reproduced within are copyright Stern School of Business.

This publication is provided "as is", without warranty of any kind, either express or implied. The author and Snarkolicious Press assume no liability for errors or omissions in this publication or other documents which are referenced or linked to this publication. While we certainly hope that you will be successful in your quest for admission to an MBA program, we cannot offer any promises that you will be, whether or not you adopt the advice provided herein. In no event shall Snarkolicious Press or its authors, principals, subsidiaries, partners, or owners be liable for any special, incidental, indirect or consequential damages of any kind, or any damages whatsoever, arising out of or in conjunction with the use or performance of this information. Applicants to any graduate program or university should verify the school's policies, application requirements, processes, procedures, and other criteria. This publication could include technical or other inaccuracies or typographical errors. Changes are periodically added to the information herein; these changes will be incorporated into new editions of this publication. Thus, different versions or formats of this publication may include different information.

Look for other *SnarkStrategies Guides* (digital and paperback) at your favorite bookseller or on the EssaySnark blahg at http://essaysnark.com.

FOLLOW ESSAYSNARK ON TWITTER!

"First, do nothing aimlessly nor without relation to the end. Secondly, relate your action to no other end except the good of human fellowship."

Marcus Aurelius

How NYU Is Different from Columbia

Let's just get this out of the way. NYU Stern is a great business school. Columbia is a great business school. They largely compete for the same students. If you're applying to Stern, chances are exceedingly high that you're applying to Columbia.

Yet Stern and Columbia could not be more different.

Beyond the fact that they both offer a top-notch MBA education in the city of New York, and both are strong in finance, there's not much more that's the same.

- They do admissions differently
- They look for (somewhat) different students
- They have different cultures – though this has changed a bit as Columbia has started focusing more on community in the past year or so

Here's a few things that Stern has that Columbia does not:

- Stern has an undergraduate program
- Stern has a part-time MBA program – the only one at a major bschool in the Northeast
- Stern has exceptional resources and support for career changers (Columbia has some, but not nearly to the same degree)
- Stern has private loan programs available to international students without the need for a U.S. co-signer.
- NYU doesn't have a real "campus" per se; it's just a collection of buildings scattered around Greenwich Village
- Stern is centrally located downtown, in Greenwich Village, close to multiple subway lines – like, almost all of them – that run on both the west side AND the east side (if you're not from New York, you may not appreciate how much this matters!)
- And, Stern has a focus on teamwork and collaboration that permeates every aspect of its student culture, from the classroom to the clubs – a focus that they look for in their candidates during their application evaluation process.

Beyond these straightforward facts, Stern also has put its money where its mouth is when it comes to diversity. Stern had a female dean (undergraduate dean Sally Blount, now dean at Kellogg) and currently has a black dean (bschool dean Peter Henry – the only black dean at a major bschool anywhere. Stern also has a special scholarship for veterans and in our opinion is more military-friendly, though Columbia has recently become more aggressive in courting vets. Finally, while Columbia has been strong for entrepreneurship for decades and is only getting stronger, we believe that NYU is at least as good for someone serious about starting up a business – and possibly in certain regards, Stern has the edge culturally for entrepreneurs.

Don't get the 'Snark wrong, we love Columbia. However despite the implication embedded some odd phrasing of an essay question last year where they claimed that they are at the center of Manhattan, Columbia is not the only game in town in New York City. Some have even opined that these days, NYU has a school of business that's just as good as, if not better than, Columbia University does. In terms of quality of education and opportunities that NYU Stern can offer in certain fields – entrepreneurship, social venture, and yes, finance – EssaySnark would have to agree.

If you're interested in more specialized fields like media and entertainment or luxury goods, then it's probably a toss-up. Both these schools are winners. You'll need to do more research on your own to see which is the better fit.

The biggest drawback with Stern? **It does not have the same clout.** This is true both as you head West in the U.S., and to a greater extent when you travel overseas, particularly to Asia. The Stern name is strong, but NYU has less brand recognition than any Ivy League school. Columbia is typically held in higher regard based on reputation factors alone. Even Johnson, with an significantly lower-ranked program, is sometimes considered more impressive in certain circles simply due to the prestige and name recognition of Cornell University.

EssaySnark doesn't think that a school should be dissed just because there's no ivy growing on its walls. We're happy to see – by the fact that you purchased this guide – that you feel the same. This *SnarkStrategies Guide* will walk you through the strengths of Stern and point out the few weaknesses. We'll give you a tour of their admissions processes and talk about how you can position yourself effectively. And yes, we'll offer some guidelines and dos and don'ts on which question to choose for Essay 2 – with a lot of discussion of the Personal Expression essay, which has been a mainstay in the application process at NYU for years and years, and which we would encourage you to consider tackling.

What's the same with both Stern and Columbia? Average graduate salaries – they're about $100k at both schools. Where does Stern come in under Columbia? Just slightly, on the cost of tuition, though the gap narrowed in the most recent year. For 2014-'15, tuition and fees are $64,628 per year at Stern – which is 3,600 more than last year. These base expenses are over $66,707 if you're getting an uptown MBA. This was a more marked difference in the prior academic year. Also if you're comparing cost estimates for Columbia and NYU, you should recognize that they're adding different numbers to get to a total.

An often overlooked point: Most of these figures are estimates, and the amount that an individual actually incurs is discretionary. The main reason for these estimates is use in lending; you will only be able to qualify for student loans up to the amount that your school estimates in tuition and expenses. So in fact, it's to your benefit for the school to have a little padding in there. That's why we're not too concerned with the fact that NYU's total first-year student budget tops out at almost $102,000 – though certainly that's a number that can take your breath away. Our sense is that Columbia may be lowballing some of their figures to keep their estimate down. Their first-year number if about $96,500. For years, Columbia has been infamous for being the most expensive MBA in the U.S. (which means it's probably the most expensive in the world). It appears that they're trying to let that honor fall to one of their competitors now but still, both of these schools are shockingly expensive. Pay attention to these facts as you start your quest for admission.

> Since we're talking numbers: Cost of tuition to complete a part-time MBA at NYU is about $115,000 (this does not include any type of living expenses, but you should be able to cover those easily enough if you're keeping your job while pursuing the MBA).
>
> The 22-month Executive MBA at NYU is about $170,000 all-in; this is a so-called "white glove" program where the administration takes care of everything for the students, including buying their books ahead of time (!), which allows the busy executive pursuing her studies to have one less thing to worry about.

Another similarity between Columbia and NYU's full-time MBAs, and one that actually matters in your application? The way they ask about career goals. We'll go into detail on that in this *Guide*.

Even more important is this little-known fact: **NYU has rolling admissions.** You probably knew that Columbia does, but many people are unaware that NYU does, too. You can apply to NYU as soon as their application opens up, and yes, they'll start reading your app and processing it through well before the deadline. At NYU, the "deadlines" are really more like "guidelines." That's discussed starting on page 6.

What else is the same with these two schools? *The amount of work you'll need to put into an application to have a real chance at either school.*

These are both super-competitive programs. Applying to either is not for the faint of heart. Be prepared for some real work ahead.

What you won't get here

As with the other *SnarkStrategies Guides*, we're not going to tell you what you should write in your Stern essays. We won't even give much in the way of examples for the Personal Expression essay. Call us purists, or prudists, or just plain persnickety, but we happen to think it's important that you craft your own strategy and content for your bschool essays. We will tell you what's been done before – like, a *lot* before – so that you can possibly rethink an approach that may come off as too clichéd. The disadvantage that the applicant has is she's going through this process for the very first time; how is a Brave Supplicant to know what others typically do with their essays? That's one way we can add value, and hopefully inspire one or two of you to dig deeper and come up with something stronger than perhaps you would have done on your own.

But if you're looking for a "do this, don't do that, say this, don't say that" type of cheat-sheet approach to your essays, EssaySnark is bound to disappoint. We don't need to write bschool essays; we already went through this process, and got in, and graduated. Now it's your turn to come up with the goods. You're the one who the Stern adcom wants to know about; it's your ideas that need to flow forth on the page. We're not going to tell you what to write.

We will, of course, guide you on how to approach things, with an eye towards presenting the best of yourself in a way that will resonate with the adcoms. We wish you the best in this process, Brave Supplicant!

Table of Contents

What Is Stern Known for?..1

What's Important at Stern..2

The NYU Langone Part-Time MBA...4

Full-Time MBA Admissions at NYU Stern...5
    Stern and rolling admissions...6
    Notification dates...7
    Interviewing at Stern 8
    Stern and the waitlist..9
    Stern rejection letters..11

Your Profile and Stern..13
    Stern and the GMAT 13
    Stern and the GPA...17
    Stern Summer Start 18

Your Stern Strategy..19
    Do you have to visit Stern before applying?..20
    Efficient Multi-School Strategies...21

The NYU Essay Questions..25

Career Goals and Stern..27
    EssaySnark's career goals exercise..27

Essay 1: Professional Aspirations...36
    Stern Essay 1 Strategy: Identify which option for Essay 2...............................36
    How to structure Stern Essay 1..39

Essay 2 Option A: Your Two Paths...44

Essay 2 Option B: Personal Expression..45
    Some Dos and Don'ts for Stern Personal Expression..48

What to Do Next..51

What Is Stern Known for?

NYU has particular strength in the fields of:

- Finance — as you would expect, given the close proximity to Wall Street — way closer than Columbia! Stern has strong ties to the investment banks as well as to hedge funds, private equity, and VC.

- Consulting — Stern sent 23% of its Class of 2013 into consulting and has relationships with the best firms in the world.

- Economics — Stern has a strong bench of economists, including rockstar Professor Nouriel Roubini. He was one of the few who predicted the subprime crisis before it happened, though at the time, nobody was listening. You'll find Professor Roubini on Twitter and CNBC as often as you will find him in class.

- Media & Entertainment — to be expected, given their location. The other schools with exceptionally strong programs in this area are Columbia and to some degree Berkeley-Haas and UCLA.

- Entrepreneurship — all types of ventures, tech and otherwise, including a growing specialization in family business.

- Social Venture and Non-Profit — an increasing area of focus, giving longstanding non-profit powerhouse school Yale a run for its money in terms of initiatives and programs.

- Luxury Goods — one of the few programs offering this specialty anywhere, though Columbia also has significant resources and opportunities (as does Harvard, and some European schools).

- Cutting-edge fields like Big Data (Business Analytics) and Social Media Marketing, and super niche areas like urbanization. Stern has announced concentrations and even new majors in these areas in recent years. Compared to its peers, NYU is a school that tends to be well ahead of the curve when it comes to trends and important business and societal developments reflected in the curriculum.

These are just a few of the areas and disciplines that Sternies are focusing on these days. Above all, NYU is a general management program, and as with other strong programs, you can do a multitude of things coming out with a Stern MBA. We'll let you discover the details about each of these areas through your own research, but they're the broad categories that this school has a special expertise in.

What's Important at Stern

Since you've already started to do your research, you should be able to easily identify the following elements and qualities as very important at this school:

- Intelligence (IQ)
- Emotional Intelligence (EQ) – includes *ethics* and *humility* and also an element of *flexibility*
- Leadership
- Creativity

These traits are evident through the language Stern uses on their website, and they're paramount in what they're looking for in their candidates. You don't necessarily have to emphasize each one of these traits separately in your application, however you should have an awareness of them, so that you can highlight them where appropriate. Dean Henry wants Stern alumni to be "servant leaders." This isn't something you'll hear at many other business schools. NYU Admissions is screening for these qualities within the application process.

Essay 2's Personal Expression option, for example, is not about evaluating how artistic you are. It is more about showing the adcom your EQ – which is also what Your Two Paths can show.

A quick note on that Personal Expression option: **This essay is a chance for you to showcase who you are.** And, it's a way for you to demonstrate how you think. Stern is always interested to see how candidates interpret the instructions. You're given a clean slate with that. What will you do with it?

Even if you think you don't have a creative bone in your body, you might want to try your hand at something visual for Essay 2. In other words, skip Option A, and also forego the written alternative for Option B. Do a non-written piece – a *thing* of some kind. It can still be electronic and uploadable (or thumbdrive-able), it doesn't have to be something you package up in a box and ship by FedEx – though if you send anything to the admissions office, we do recommend using FedEx or some other trackable service.

The main point is you should try to move past the essay as your primary means of communicating yourself.

The big exception to this advice is if you came into the essay-writing process already having two possible plans for your future career mapped out – then, the Your Two Paths question makes a lot of sense. But EssaySnark's suggestion? Go with Personal Expression if you can. We'll explain why and give a lot more guidance later on in this *Guide*, we just wanted to mention it so you can start to stew over your choices.

Back to Stern and what they're about. Perhaps the most important aspect at this school is *community*. They want to see how you've engaged. And it's one of the most important aspects of your profile that you'll need to highlight and leverage throughout your application. We'll talk more about this – but just keep it in mind (and just for the record: the emphasis on *community* is the major difference between Stern and its uptown neighbor).

This leads us right off the bat to:

Snarky Strategy #1

> *Community* matters at Stern.
> Figure out what "community" means to them, and to your bschool experience – and figure out what it means to you.
> Then show that in your essays.

We'll be talking more about community and Stern later in this *Guide*, and you should be focusing on this as you continue your research into the school.

One final huge benefit to mention, that Stern has and Columbia only recently became marginally competitive with?

Having a beautiful website that's well organized, and with useful information throughout.

Look for the Directors' Tips on Stern's site. Listen to the audio clips. There's a wealth of advice available and free for the having.

The NYU Langone Part-Time MBA

The bulk of this *SnarkStrategies Guide* is focused on the full-time candidate applying for the standard two-year MBA. However, Stern has an excellent part-time option that's viable for many. The Stern part-time MBA is a great idea for anyone who's got a great job that they don't want to walk away from for two years. It's slightly less great for someone who wants to do a radical career change, though that's certainly also possible through the part-time program.

Here are some basics about Stern's part-time program for employed individuals:

- Stern accepts around 450 part-time students into the Fall program and another 300 in the Spring, for a total of 2,000 students going through the Langone program at any one time. This compares to about 800 total in the full-time track (400 full-time students per graduating class). The average part-timer completes her MBA in three years, though it's possible to get through it quicker, and some students opt to go more slowly. It's often easier to get into the January start simply because there's less competition.

- There are three possible tracks among the two NYU campus locations: Manhattan Weeknights, Manhattan Weekends, or Westchester Weeknights. You must apply to a specific track, and if accepted, you must stay in that track for a year before you're allowed to switch, and then only if spots open up in another track. The Weeknights option typically means two nights of class per week. The Weekends option is both classes the same day, one Saturday morning and the other Saturday afternoon.

- Not all specializations are offered in the weekend track, and not all classes are offered at the Westchester campus. You can stay flexible and apply to both campuses together, but that's a commitment; if you're accepted to Westchester then you'd have to go to Westchester. Some students commute from long distances (by plane) for the weekend option, and it would be feasible to do that at either campus.

- Langone has one application date for January and one for August, though they will evaluate applications submitted past that date until the class is full. This means that they're often still accepting applications for the August start in late summer. Yes, there can be a chance to slip in under the wire for Stern P/T.

- Interviews are not required for admission to the Langone program (they are required for admission to the full-time program).

- It is not possible to switch from the part-time to the full-time program, though you can accelerate your progress in the part-time program if you wish, by taking three classes at once instead of the standard two, and/or by taking short intensives in between semesters.

- Many electives at the Stern Manhattan campus are integrated with both full-time and part-time students. The professors at Stern generally teach in both programs, so it is the same MBA regardless of which schedule you're on. Part-time students can take daytime classes on a space-available basis. Part-time students get priority for the evening classes over any full-time student who may want to take it.

If you're already in the New York area and you're committed to going to NYU – and particularly if your profile is a little weak in either the GPA or GMAT – and, you're up for the intensity that getting your MBA while maintaining a full-time job involves, then you might consider the Langone option. There is less competition for this program and a decent candidate should have a relatively "easy" time getting an offer ("easy" is in quotes because it's never easy to get into any top MBA program). The school is somewhat looser in its admissions criteria simply because they have a lot of seats to fill each year and not as many candidates interested. In fact, the criteria is so much looser that 10% of Langone students have a GMAT score under 620.

If you're looking to switch careers, the full-time MBA would be an easier path, though it's not impossible to change careers through the Langone program. The most important difference is that Stern does not allow part-time students to participate in on-campus recruiting. Those recruiters – and jobs – are reserved for the full-timers, although Stern does provide a dedicated career services office for the part-time cohort, with some specific finance and consulting firms offering career events just for Langone students.

From here on out, this *SnarkStrategies Guide* focuses on admissions to the full-time MBA, though a Langone candidate will also find much of value here. Just be sure to check the deadlines and essay questions for Langone, since they are quite different from the full-time program's dates and requirements – notably, Langone applicants still have a mandatory Personal Expression essay, and just one deadline per intake.

Full-Time MBA Admissions at NYU Stern

Here are a few details about the processes and policies with the full-time MBA at the NYU Stern School of Business.

You may have already noticed that Stern has four rounds. This is pretty unique these days – in fact, one of the few other schools that had four rounds – Berkeley Haas – reduced them down to three last year.

The big drawback with how Stern operated previously with a November Round 1 was that applicants wouldn't hear back until February on their apps, which is very very late in comparison to other schools. Now they are on equal footing with their peers in terms of decision timing: You apply in October, you get at least a preliminary response by December (you're cut loose with a "no" or you're in the interview cycle, at minimum).

And, Stern still has an advantage of a Fall application deadline that's off the standard cycle at other schools. Tuck has a November deadline too. There's actually a lot of similarities between NYU and Tuck in terms of great school, great community, but that's a separate conversation. These November deadlines are a gift to Brave Supplicants everywhere: They are less competitive than other schools' Round 2s that hit in January, and they come at a point in the admissions cycle where it's easier to do a great job on the apps.

With NYU (or Tuck), you can stress out and scramble for all the other Round 1 deadlines in early October, feeling panicked and pressured as you apply to the other schools on your list – and then you can relax and unwind for a bit, and chill out and de-stress for the rest of the month... before realizing on November 1st that you have just two more weeks till NYU is due, and starting the freak-out all over again.

Side note: It's rare that we see Brave Supplicants actually getting everything done early for a school, regardless of how late that school's deadline is. Whatever application you're planning for, and whatever month it currently is, EssaySnark exhorts you to *start now*.

A very big advantage of the Stern November deadline is that it gives you additional opportunities to come to campus, learn what they're about, and interact with the student community. Stern is also on the road throughout the fall, so if you can't come to New York, NYU will come to you. Stern is serious about candidates getting to know them before applying, and the November deadline gives you no excuses.

Stern and rolling admissions

As mentioned earlier, Stern and Columbia are quasi-alike in one area of their admissions processes: They both do things on a "rolling" basis. How this works in practice is quite different between the two schools but the essential fact remains: Applying early at either of these schools is highly recommended.

The main reason that Stern publishes any deadline at all is for your benefit, so that you have a date to motivate yourself with. Stern processes applications as they are received and they release decisions as they are made. The main reason that they made a change and introduced an October Round 1 in 2013 was to standardize among their peer schools. You can submit well ahead of Stern's Round 1 deadline – or in between rounds, or even after a deadline. They're not strict about these things at all (that's not how it works at other schools).

Snarky Strategy #2

Take advantage of rolling admissions: Apply early.

Our recommendation is to apply to Stern at the earliest opportunity – both in terms of hitting their first round, assuming you really like them and aren't making the classic mistake of thinking that they're a "safety school." Applying at the earliest opportunity also means applying before the published round deadline. This will give you greatest advantage – provided that your profile is strong and you've done your homework in how to position yourself.

That being said: "Don't rush to receive bad news," as the Stern admissions director says. Make sure that your application is as strong as it can be before submitting it. If you need to come in a few days past the deadline – or a few weeks – that could still be better than pushing in a flawed application.

Notification dates

Another point about Stern's process: They release decisions as they are made. This helps explain their use of the "Initial Notification Dates" which are posted on their website. Those dates are your worst-case scenario dates.

If you're being denied outright, then that's as long as you'll have to wait to know your fate. If you're going to be interviewed, you probably will get word of that before the notification date. Depending on how early your interview invite comes and how quickly you get yourself to NYC to do the interview, then there's even a chance you could get your final decision (accept/waitlist/reject) before the Initial Notification Date.

Just don't mistake the Initial Notification Date for a decision date; they're not necessarily the same. If you've heard nothing from Stern up to the time the notification date rolls around, it's less likely to be good news when it finally comes – though you still could be invited to interview even at that late stage.

Stern admissions told us recently that they're working on reducing cycle times in application processing, because they know how stressful it is for you Brave Supplicants. It's possible that you will experience the benefits of this in the coming admissions season.

Post-interview decisions

You can expect to get a final decision (accept/waitlist/reject) about three weeks after you complete your interview with Stern admissions. This is why it's to your advantage to get the interview completed as soon as possible after your invite.

Since we're on the subject of interviews:

Interviewing at Stern

Interviews are required for admission to the full-time Stern program, but that doesn't mean that all candidates are interviewed. Instead, interviews are conducted by invitation only – and in fact, the Stern approach *is to only interview candidates for whom they feel there's a spot.*

This means that if the adcom likes what they see in your app, they'll ask you to meet with them for an in-depth conversation about your interest in their program. They won't admit anyone without the interview, and they won't interview someone that they're feeling mediocre about. About 70% of candidates invited to interview end up being admitted. That's higher than at most schools.

What happens more at Stern than at some other schools is that they might invite you to join the waitlist BEFORE interviewing. They don't want to dedicate the resources required on their end to interview you unless they feel confident that there's a spot available if they decide to accept you, and they also (kindly, in our opinion) don't want to raise false hopes, nor have you incur unnecessary expense, in having you come to campus to interview if there is little chance of an admit.

Interview invites begin going out about to Stern full-time applicants usually about a month after the deadline, all the way up to the notification date. The timing of when your invitation comes through has nothing to do with the strength of your candidacy – though it may have something to do with how early you applied.

The biggest difference with a Stern interview compared to other places? They are generally done on site, in New York, by a member of the Stern admissions team. Stern calls their admissions people "trained assessors of talent" and EssaySnark does feel that any school whose adcom does its own interviews is at an advantage in the selection process.

With a NYU application, you're strongly encouraged to get yourself to New York for the interview. Stern admissions also travels to a limited number of international locations, usually in the December – January timeframe. If you just can't pull off a trip to NYC, you must instead travel to one of these hub cities. They very rarely grant requests for phone interviews, typically only in the case of actively-deployed military. You probably shouldn't bother applying to Stern if you're not able to come to one of these locations for the interview process.

You also need to prepare for the Stern interview differently than you might for an alumni interview. Your Stern interviewer will have read your entire application. Studied it, no less. They take their jobs seriously and really work to get to know the candidates (not that other schools don't, but they go the extra mile at NYU).

In fact, many people report coming away from a Stern interview with a folder that the admissions team has compiled with all the specific clubs and activities that they believe the candidate would be interested in – tailored specifically to their profile. These are not just the standardized pieces of marketing collateral that everyone gets; each folder is constructed custom for each specific applicant. They go that far in understanding who you are. This is why it's so important for you to go the extra mile in learning about them, before you apply – you want to extend this courtesy to them if you expect them to respond in kind.

Preparing for a Stern interview is beyond scope of this essay guide, however we go into a detailed methodology for getting ready for this type of open interview in the *EssaySnark MBA Interviewing Guide*, available in The Bookstore at http://essaysnark.com/bookstore/ .

Important note: If you're invited to interview for the full-time program, they ask that you bring official copies of your transcripts to your interview appointment. They need an official transcript from every college or university you've ever attended, for any length of time, regardless of whether you received a degree there or not. Unofficial copies may be uploaded into the online application. If you anticipate that it will take some time for your undergraduate institution to send over official versions, you may want to request them in advance.

Stern and the waitlist

We need to alert you to a pattern that we've observed over many years: Stern seems to put a lot of people on the waitlist. We already mentioned one reason for this, that they will waitlist someone before an interview if they're not certain if they have room. Another reason that we have surmised for the higher number of waitlisted candidates is because Stern's yield is relatively low compared to other top programs.

A school's *yield* is the percent of applicants that accepts the schools offer. Yield is the ratio of how many candidates the school accepts, that also accept *them*. A low yield means that the school must accept a lot more applicants than will actually end up enrolling there as students. Stern loses a high number of accepted applicants via attrition to other schools. If you're accepted to both NYU and to Yale... a certain number will choose Yale. Multiple that out by the infinite number of permutations of who applies to which combination of schools, and you can understand the problem Stern faces.

Because of this, Stern seems more reluctant to give an outright 'no' to a lot of borderline applicants than they otherwise might. They need to keep a good number of Brave

Supplicants hanging around while they wait and see what the outcomes will be for those applicants who they did accept. And those outcomes are often not known until very late in the season. Like, March. Or April. Or even sometimes August.

It can be excruciating to end up on the waitlist. You're in a veritable limbo, a no-man's land. You're not accepted, but you might be... but you just don't know. It is incredibly demoralizing. You're being told you're not quite good enough – what does that mean? It can be even worse than a straight-up rejection. At least with a rejection, you can mourn your losses and move on.

In our experience, Brave Supplicants are often inordinately surprised at a waitlist outcome – for some reason, these are often the ones who expected to sail right through. Typically these are the types who EssaySnark has been warning for weeks that there could be issues with their candidacy (like, low GMAT, low GPA, unclear career goals), yet they scoffed us aside and plowed ahead with an application and submitted it despite our reservation. And then the non-answer answer comes, and they rear back in shock. And *now* they're ready to scramble.

"I'll do anything, tell me what to do!"

And we say to ourselves, *Damn, it sure would've been nice if you said this three months ago when we told you to retake the GMAT.*

And so what we say to them is, "Maybe you should retake the GMAT." Or take a class, to offset the poor academics. Or whatever it was we'd been suggesting all along.

And sometimes they do. And often, those are the ones who are then offered a spot.

Stern is open to getting updates from you if you're on the waitlist – provided you don't stalk them. Their advice to candidates who are waitlisted is to "be aggressive about what you can do to make yourself better." Just don't be aggressive with the admissions people! This is a time for your EQ to shine through.

We've seen this work out in plenty a BSer's favor. The waitlist is not a death sentence. If you want more guidance on how to navigate the waitlist at Stern or any school, we've written a whole book on that topic alone: *EssaySnark's Guide to Getting off the Waitlist* available in the Bookstore on essaysnark.com.

Yes, NYU puts a lot of people on the waitlist – but we've also seen them *admit* a lot of people from the waitlist. And, they give very, very clear instructions to waitlisted candidates on what they can do to have a chance of an offer.

Stern does *not* however offer feedback, neither to waitlisted candidates nor to rejected candidates. Only a few schools do. Stern's position is, if you can't self-assess and figure out what went wrong in your application, then are you really prepared to be a leader in the business world? That being said: Applying earlier in the admissions season is always smart;

sometimes qualified candidates are turned way in the springtime. If that's when you applied, then the situation may be a little more complex.

The moral of this story: If you've had an interaction with EssaySnark whereby we suggested that maybe your profile is flawed, you might want to spend more time upfront, fixing those issues, before submitting your application to NYU. It is much more gratifying — and way less stressful — to get admitted the first time through, than to have to go through a tormented scramble of trying to correct the flaws later when you're in waitlist wasteland and the way forward is far from clear.

Stern rejection letters

Hopefully you never discover the truth of what we're about to say firsthand — but we wanted to tell you about it, just in case. It provides an opportunity for you.

Stern handles rejections in a different way than most schools. They send different reject notices to applicants depending on whether or not they want the candidate to reapply. London Business School also does this, but most schools do not.

Every now and then, Stern sees a candidate they like, but who they are not willing to admit just yet, based on correctable flaws in the profile. In those cases, the Stern adcom will send a signal to the candidate in the rejection, based on how they phrase their letter.

These examples are from a couple years back and so the language may change with the upcoming admissions season. However, these are the letters that Stern has used in these two cases in the past:

Standard Stern Denial

```
Dear _____,

The Admissions Committee has completed its review of your
application to the NYU Stern MBA program. After careful
consideration, we are unable to offer you admission.

While the Committee recognizes the high aspirations and
unique qualities of all of our applicants, we are in the
difficult position of being able to offer admission to only a
small percentage of the many individuals who apply to our
program. Our decisions are based on a holistic process in
which we evaluate each applicant's academic profile,
professional achievements, and personal characteristics.

We appreciate your interest in NYU Stern and regret that we
are unable to offer you a place in the class. We wish you all
the best in the future.
```

Stern Denial with the Door Open

> Dear _____,
>
> The Admissions Committee has completed its review of your application to NYU Stern. After careful consideration of your application and credentials, we are unable to offer you admission. We would like to encourage you to reapply in the future.
>
> While the Committee saw positive qualities in your application, there were also some areas that could be strengthened. To maximize career planning, class participation, and the overall learning experience, we have found that our most successful candidates have the following characteristics:
>
> - A strong record of professional success and leadership, with recommendation letters that support these qualities
>
> - Demonstrated potential for academic success, as shown through impressive undergraduate work and standardized test scores
>
> - Focused and well-defined career goals that match our program offerings
>
> - Well-written, insightful essays and excellent communication skills
>
> - Overall personal and professional maturity and motivation
>
> We hope that your interest in the NYU Stern School of Business will continue and that you will reapply to NYU Stern in the future. For information about the abbreviated reapplication process, please visit our website. We appreciate your interest in NYU Stern. We wish you all the best in the future.

Again, these are the versions that had been in effect in past years (people had posted them on an applicant forum in 2012). They may change this year.

Hopefully you never receive either version. If you do, regardless of which version you get, you should never hesitate to reapply to Stern if you're in love with them. Make sure you have improved your profile, do a better job on your essays, and give it a go. They're open to checking you out again, and they'll give you a fair review the second time through. If they included some of the above language in their initial denial letter, then you may have a better chance than others. Be sure to reapply in Round 1 of the next admissions season, to reinforce your position of how motivated you are to go to Stern, and you'll have the best chance possible.

Your Profile and Stern

Let's break down some of the elements of the application so you can see how you stack up against what Stern is looking for.

Emphasis on Significant Work Experience

With an average age of 28 in the full-time program, Stern is one of the "older" MBA programs. This is even more so when you consider the Langone program: many of the part-timers are in their 30s, and their average age is closer to 29 (the range is from one to twenty years of work experience). Most Sternies have around five years of work experience.

Stern will consider an application from someone much younger, however you'd need to not only express how you're at the right stage of your life to benefit from the MBA, but you'd also need to show how you've achieved a lot already – beyond what others your age have. And, your GMAT and GPA likely will need to be higher than someone who's got a more standard work experience profile. The adcom will be looking for more from you if you apply at a younger age.

This is not to say that you shouldn't give it a shot, but you'll have your work cut out for you. If you're determined to go to bschool right now, then maybe you'll want to look into other schools that are more accommodating of younger candidates (Harvard, Chicago, and perhaps MIT are some that are a little more flexible).

NYU can be very welcoming for "older" candidates who have five years or more of experience and a solid career progression. At least three years of significant work experience is recommended before seriously considering Stern for your MBA.

Stern and the GMAT

Stern cares about your GMAT. Most schools do, but Stern really does. Part of this may be due to their concentration of finance folks – anyone recruiting for a job on Wall Street has got to bring the goods.

EssaySnark is talking about the GMAT here, even though Stern does accept the GRE. Most candidates take the GMAT, and it's what the schools publish their student averages on. You can substitute "GRE" anywhere we say "GMAT" in this *Guide* though you should also read the posts on the EssaySnark blahg about the differences between the tests, and some advantages to the GMAT.

Believe it or not, your GMAT score will be a factor of consideration in the recruiting process for many companies recruiting at your business school. Stern wants its students to be successful in the job market, and they want their recruiters to be impressed with the quality of graduates coming out. One way to ensure this is to use the GMAT as a weighty part of the evaluation process in admissions.

Now, before you get all huffy, Stern is not evaluating *you* on the basis of just a test score. You are much more than that. You're a person, and you cannot be distilled down to just a number. We know that. They know that.

Instead, they – and other top schools – use the GMAT as a proxy. What the GMAT score can tell a school is:

a) Can this person handle numbers (quant)

b) Can this person deal with English? (verbal)

c) Can this person string together coherent sentences into a reasonably logical argument? (AWA)

d) Can this person make inferences and combine disparate pieces of data into conclusions that make sense? (IR)

And even more importantly:

e) Is this person dedicated to the process?

There's even a sixth thing:

f) Does this person have the self-awareness to evaluate their own potential?

You see, a GMAT score does way more than simply tell them if you can factor an equation. The *history* of GMAT scores – yes, the schools see your full history – can tell them if you're serious about this whole MBA business. If you took the GMAT once and did great, great. If you took the GMAT once and did just OK... were you satisfied with that? Or did you try again? And if you took the GMAT and you fumbled, what did you do from there?

The frequency of test attempts and even the timing of them can actually reveal quite a bit to the adcom.

Stern looks at *everything*. Stern wants to see you succeed. Stern is actually quite liberal in its policies around retesting the GMAT, too. They'll keep in mind an upcoming test date and delay their decision until you submit a new score.

Say the application deadline is approaching. Say you're going back and forth about your GMAT score. You know you can do better, but you don't want to delay your application to the next round. Stern will let you apply at the current deadline, and you can tell them about when your next test date is scheduled. They will set your app aside until you send in the new score, and then proceed with their evaluation. Most other schools are not nearly so accommodating, and may decide on your application with the original score you submitted.

So, what's a good GMAT score for Stern?

The average GMAT score for the NYU Class of 2015 is 721 – one point higher than the Class of 2014. This remains among the highest of the very best programs. Only Harvard, Stanford, and Wharton are higher. In fact, the average GMAT for Columbia Business School is a whopping five points lower, at 716 – which is a very big difference, given that it's a bigger program and can more easily absorb a wider range of scores without affecting the mean.

The 80% range for accepted students at Stern is 680 to 760, which is a similar tight band as some other schools have. Columbia has an identical 80% range, but we can tell from the average that Columbia is accepting more people with scores on the lower end. NYU has higher standards.

If you're below a 680 total GMAT score, it may be tough to get an offer at NYU. Not impossible, but you're making it hard on yourself. In fact, if you're below a 700, you have more challenges than you might expect.

To offer more granularity on what might be acceptable: A 35 verbal and 47 quant would be bare minimums that we're comfortable with for Stern. That combination should put you in their 80%-range, with a 680 or so total score. This is the very lowest-bottom level and it makes us nervous, but yes, we've seen people get in with a score around there. To be clear, we're not condoning that score. A higher score will help you *a lot*. But you're in the realm of possibility if you've got a score breakdown like that, particularly with an early-season app.

Stern does have a preference for higher GMAT scores. We don't want to mislead you. We're only telling you about what could let you squeak by. Those numbers are clearly not ideal for this school.

If your GMAT score is weighted mostly on one side or the other – say, a 680 made up of a good verbal and lower quant – you might still be OK at Stern. Because of the strength of the Summer Start program discussed below (page 18), Stern might be more open to accepting you than another bschool would be that is more intent on seeing a balanced GMAT. As with everything, it depends on the entirety of your profile.

If you're feeling nervous about your GMAT score, and you think you can do better, it's perfectly fine to submit your application with your current score and tell the adcom about your plans to re-test. You should schedule your next test date, and then in the optional essay, let the adcom know when that will be. They will accept your application in the current round, but set it aside until you send in the new score. Of course, the risk here is that you don't raise the score – or that you even do worse.

If that happens, just inform them of the results in an email (you should probably also fax in the unofficial score report you got on the day of the test). Don't neglect to follow-up with them though! Your application will be in limbo until you do. If your score is borderline, they're likely to appreciate the fact that you've attempted to bring it up – even if you fail to nudge it by much.

You should only go with this strategy if you're committed to retesting and improving. Just going through the motions in an effort to make them *think* you're serious about it is not likely to win you anything.

A finally note: A too-low GMAT score alone sometimes seems to land lots of applicants on the Stern waitlist. We talked about the waitlist earlier; it's a real thing at Stern. More than once, EssaySnark has seen otherwise-qualified candidates end up waitlisted at first, only to be offered admission fairly quickly once they retested and sent in a higher score. We already covered the Stern waitlist earlier, so this is just to reiterate: *GMAT matters.*

The AWA matters, too

There's a myth in some GMAT test-prep circles that the AWA is meaningless on the GMAT. That is just not true. While the schools do not bother reporting average AWA scores for their students, it's not because it's immaterial.

At NYU, if your AWA is too low, they may ask you to go through a special writing workshop before classes begin (at an additional cost). We haven't seen Stern be fanatical about the AWA score, however it would help you to be at a 5.0 or above.

The IR is taking on increasing importance

Schools are still collecting their data on IR and student performance, and some are seeing that the integrated reasoning section of the GMAT has a strong correlation to first-year grades – more so than the other sections of the test do. While the IR is still not a requirement for applying to Stern or other schools, you should recognize what it shows about you and strive to do well on that portion of the test, too. If you originally tested awhile back and you didn't have to do Integrated Reasoning at the time, you do not need to retake the test just to have an IR score to report.

However, if your score is too far out of date (over three years old), then it's becoming less useful for the schools as a measure of your current skills, so you may want to consider retesting even if your GMAT is technically still valid.

Stern and the GPA

NYU has a remarkably high average GPA for its students. The Classes of 2014 and 2015 both reported an impressive 3.51 – this is almost as high as Stanford's. Most schools considered peers of NYU have an average undergrad GPA of only around 3.4, which is a very big difference. Along with the realities of the GMAT that we just discussed, this tells us how much Stern values academics and book smarts in its admissions decisions.

In fact, we need to lay this out for you very clearly: NYU Stern is not a school that is very flexible on GPA. We very rarely see a Brave Supplicant with a GPA under 3.0 who even get invited to interview at this school.

We had one guy with a poor GPA get waitlisted pre-interview but he was later released with no offer. The lowest GPA we've seen from a standard-profile BSer who made it into Stern was 3.1 on the U.S. 4.0 scale – and that was as a reapplicant, after she took significant steps to fix the weaknesses for the second time through.

We did see someone with a lower GPA get in but he had mitigating factors in his profile that helped him – and he was initially waitlisted, and then only admitted after he retook the GMAT and got a 720. It was definitely not a straightforward process for him.

Obviously they do admit people with lower GPAs – EssaySnark doesn't have access to the entire set of data of admitted Sternies – but those cases are few and far between. If your GPA is low, then you'll definitely want a high GMAT score, and some compelling stories elsewhere in your profile to show why you're the right candidate for this program.

A Snarky Caveat

> If you want to go to Stern, don't kid yourself about your GPA. If you did poorly in college, then take action on it now – before you apply.

If your transcripts from undergrad are a little rough around the edges, the standard EssaySnark advice applies: To take a class before you apply to bschool in order to shore up your profile. EssaySnark talks about low GPA ad nauseum on the blahg. Here's a post to start with: http://essaysnark.com/2010/05/omg-2-posts-in-2-days.html.

Taking a class like statistics or calculus is ideal. Many schools would appreciate this addition to strengthen a profile. In such a case, it's definitely more useful for them to see a grade from a completed class, than simply a statement that the class is in progress (though even the latter is helpful if it's all you've got and timing is an issue). If you can, plan ahead and take a class if you feel your profile needs a boost.

It doesn't matter if you take an in-person classroom-based class or an online class; they just want to see that it's a challenging course covering the appropriate material. UC-Berkeley Extension has some self-paced courses (see http://extension.berkeley.edu/math/selfpaced.html) that may be perfect, or if you're in the New York area, you can go to NYU Continuing Education, or PACE or CUNY or any other local school. We've heard that UCLA also has some online course offerings that are convenient and appropriate for pre-MBA fixing-a-transcript work.

You'll also want to submit an optional essay with some explanation around what was going on for you in college and what steps you've taken to address this gap in the profile. Again, look to the EssaySnark blahg for posts on what to say (and not to say) in this important deliverable to the adcom.

Stern Summer Start

One topic that's not part of the admissions process per se but deserves discussion here is a pre-term program offered at Stern called Summer Start. This is a special curriculum that they make available to students on a case-by-case, invitation-only basis. Stern Summer Start is designed for the otherwise-qualified student who may have some weaknesses in their skillset, either on the quant side, or sometimes on the English language side, in speaking or writing. Sometimes they offer Summer Start to international students who have never spent time in the U.S. or another Western country; those coming from nontraditional backgrounds like teaching or the Peace Corps are also frequently invited. You'll be notified by the admissions team if they think you would benefit from this pre-term coursework.

Stern Summer Start begins in July and goes for six weeks. You would take the core statistics class in the summer program, so you'll have that out of the way, and you'll also take a couple different management and leadership courses. These are an opportunity to increase your skills and also to begin developing relationships with your peers. Assessment tests are given at the end of the program, and these are important, as they tell you – and the school – if you'll be able to manage once the full schedule of classes begins in August.

Admission to Summer Start is by invitation only, and if you are accepted to Stern and offered a spot in Summer Start, you are not obligated to do it – you can still go to NYU and start in August if you choose to pass up on the pre-term opportunity. Summer Start is also an add-on in terms of the tuition expense and requires a larger deposit to secure your spot in the incoming Stern class. However, if they offer it to you, we'd recommend you go for it. They're seeing something in your profile that they think you might need help with.

In fact, if your profile is weak in one area, you could even mention Summer Start in an essay, saying that you'd be interested in the opportunity if they offered it (if, in fact, you would be – you'd never want to say something like this if you didn't intend to accept!).

Your Stern Strategy

With your Stern application, you need to do the same as you need to do with many bschool apps: You need to explain why you want an MBA, in the context of what you want to do with the degree when you graduate. And, especially, you need to show them who you are and why you want an MBA from Stern.

This requirement of messaging is obvious in how the NYU adcom has presented their essay questions:

- **Essay 1: Professional Aspirations** (where you've been and where you want to go)

- **Essay 2: Your Two Paths** (more professional aspirations – which gives more insights into who you are) or **Personal Expression** (who you are)

With Stern's essays, we almost don't think any guidance is needed. After all, they're laying it all right out there in black and white.

Start with those labels that they've used to define each question, and look at the specific prompts they want you to answer in your essay. Many Brave Supplicants seem to overlook these titles, but they're an important signal to how to handle the questions. If you step back and examine those at a high level, you can see that the adcom is telling you what they want to know about. They want to know about your goals (essay 1), and they want to know who you are (essay 2). Maybe we're oversimplifying but it's pretty basic stuff.

And then if you examine the subquestions within each essay – question 1 in particular – then you also understand that they want to know what you know about Stern, and why you're applying there. A big part of your strategy needs to be a demonstration of why you are choosing Stern.

This "why Stern" angle and your reasons for choosing them must be clear and compelling. We'll talk about this a lot more throughout the pages of this *Guide*, but the basic idea is that "school fit" matters A LOT, and you need to pull out all the stops in convincing the adcom that you're in love with them. You need details here. You'll need to express an understanding of what Stern can offer, based on how you talk about the opportunities you'd be afforded by going there.

If you want to go to Stern for your MBA, you'll need to make it a priority to do significant research and learn about who they are and what they offer. You'll probably end up devoting significantly more time to the essays than you expect. Your application must demonstrate how you'll dive in and make a contribution – and one way to do that is to engage with the school *now*, before you even apply.

That leads us to the question that we're asked most often when someone is kicking the tires on whether to apply to this school or not.

Do you have to visit Stern before applying?

If you want to go to Stern, it wouldn't hurt to *go to Stern*. An applicant to any of the Top 20 bschools in the world would benefit from visiting that school and understanding what they're about. But there are a handful of schools in the Top 15 where it's really super important that you go visit before applying if you possibly can. NYU is in that category.

Now, it may not be quite as *mandatory* to visit NYU pre-application as it would be for, say, Tuck. (If you've read the *SnarkStrategies Guide for Tuck*, you know that EssaySnark issues a firm directive there that you HAVE to go up to Hanover, New Hampshire, to experience the place for yourself, before applying.) We're not saying you HAVE to visit Stern. But we're saying that you SHOULD.

Which other school has an essay question that directly asks you to talk about what efforts you've made to learn about them?

Answer: Just one (Ross. Berkeley used to have such a question, but they don't anymore.)

If you live anywhere on the Eastern Seaboard, they'll expect you to come to campus. It's not stated or required, but a motivated person would do so. And if you live in New York City and you haven't visited? That's pretty much inexcusable. The Stern adcom will be unimpressed with you if you don't, to say the least.

Snarky Strategy #3

If you can manage a trip to New York, it would be well worth your while to visit Stern before applying.

And who doesn't want an excuse to visit New York?!?

You can visit Columbia when you're there, too – and even potentially Wharton, and/or Harvard, and/or MIT, and/or Yale – or even Tuck. If you're applying to Tuck, you *have* to visit, so why not also include Stern in your whirlwind tour?

If you've never ever been to New York before – well, you really should try to visit at least once before you commit to attending school there for two years. It's an intense place. Some of people are absolutely miserable when they first move there. Make sure you know what you're getting into. Don't go into this thing blind.

Now if you just can't pull it off, no big deal – many people only visit for the first time when they go for their interview. As we mentioned already, you should definitely plan on going to campus for the interview.

If you can't afford any of this pre-admission travel stuff and you're putting up all sorts of objections to these suggestions we're making then we just have to ask: Are you sure you can afford the MBA? This is an expensive proposition you're undertaking, every way you look at it. If you're not in a position today to make some investment in yourself, by doing the legwork and visiting some schools, then it's hard to see how you're ready for others to make an investment in you by admitting you and funding your education through loans and possibly scholarships. We're just sayin'.

Efficient Multi-School Strategies

Every now and then, someone comes to us effusive about NYU and committed to getting in there as her top-choice favoritist school. Usually though, NYU is among a list of possible targets that the BSer is considering. Let's go over some considerations for how to prioritize Stern versus other schools, both across rounds within an entire admissions season, and also within a single round, in terms of which essays to do when.

When should you apply to Stern?

With all schools, applying in an earlier round is highly recommended. Usually that means Round 1, for a three-round school; Round 2 is typically a lot more competitive, and Round 3 should just be skipped as too much of a risk.

For Stern and other four-round schools like Tuck or Duke, you have more flexibility:

- Apply to Stern in the earliest round you can, preferably in Round 1. Round 2 would also be an advantage. These first two rounds are near-equivalent in terms of benefits for you.

- Round 3 is fine but it will be harder to stand out.

- Avoid Round 4.

Round 3 for Stern is comparable to most other schools' Round 2; it's a more competitive round, but it's no problem if that's where you end up applying. Rounds 1 and 2 will be the best bet since fewer people will be applying in those rounds, so it'll be easier to get the attention of the adcom when your app is strong, and availability will be wide open. Round 4 is to be avoided since the class will mostly be full by then, and the adcom typically only can admit the very best candidates then.

The other advantages to applying to Stern in an earlier round are that you'll hear back from them sooner, and you'll have more options for interviewing. Thus, we recommend Round 1 if possible.

When should you apply to Stern if you are also applying to Columbia?

This depends on which is your first-choice school. Obviously if Columbia is #1 then you use their Early Decision option. If you apply to Columbia Early Decision early enough, you could potentially have your final Columbia answer back before Stern Round 1 is due – though more likely, before Stern Round 2 is due. If Columbia says no in ED, then you would move to Stern as your next app – and you would have learned so much from doing the Columbia essays that your NYU application will be all that much stronger. Writing essays involves a learning curve, and your skills will improve the more essays you write.

Or: You like Columbia. But you also like Stern. You decide not to submit to Columbia Early Decision because maybe you'd rather go to Stern (or maybe you just screw up in October and don't have your Columbia act together in time for their Early Decision round). You get two chances to try for Stern before the year is out, after which you can turn your attention to Columbia and the Regular Decision application. That represents a big advantage for Stern, in giving you so many opportunities to submit, and it's a big advantage for you, in being able to take your time and apply when you're ready.

If you go for Stern's November Round 2, then you may not get a final answer from them until mid-February or later – but still, that's probably sooner than you'll get a final decision from your Columbia regular-round application (which you should submit in December at the latest – we cover those strategies in the *SnarkStrategies Guide for Columbia*). Stern notifies students as soon as they are accepted, and in the past, for the November round that often has happened in January.

Finally, we shouldn't have to say this but we will: Don't mistake Stern for an easier school to get into than some other top-ranked program. It's absolutely not. Don't treat Stern as a "safety school" in your quest for Columbia. We see too many unprepared Brave Supplicants making the ill-advised decision to slap together a Stern app while they're waiting for Columbia to let them in. Often in such cases, both schools take a pass. Take Stern seriously. They will take you seriously if you do.

The takeaway message for you? Apply to Stern when you are ready – in the earliest round that you can, Round 1 or Round 2 preferably, and ahead of the deadline if possible. Even a few days early can make a difference. At minimum, submitting before the deadline will allow you to minimize some stress and avoid the server logjams that can happen when everyone tries to submit at once, and it could also potentially help you by being ahead of the crush.

How should you manage the Stern and CBS essay writing tasks?

We talked at the beginning of this *Guide* about all the differences between NYU and Columbia. Are there similarities? Yes, there are – specifically, in how you should structure your career goals essay.

Both Columbia and NYU are asking you to present your goals from a certain perspective. The NYU essay needs to be handled much differently overall, because you need to emphasize the traits and qualities that NYU cares about.

However, the frame from which you set up your first essay should be somewhat similar between both these two schools' goals essays. This doesn't mean you can reuse your drafts from one school to the next. It does mean you need to use the same type of thinking to approach them – at least for the beginning. The two essay questions are also quite unique from each other, so don't take that advice too far.

Snarky Strategy #4

> If you're also applying to Columbia – and who isn't – then figure out your short-answer response first. Then draft Stern Essay 1, all the way through. Then go back to Columbia Essay 1.

Why? Because this will help you build out the answers to both schools' questions as efficiently as possible. You could start with Columbia first and complete those essays before starting Stern's, however the breakdown of three questions that Stern is asking in their Essay 1 will actually help you in formulating your answer to Columbia Essay 1. The disadvantage is that Stern's first essay is quite a bit longer than Columbia's, and it's usually easier to build out a shorter essay, than to try and pare back a longer draft to fit a more limited length requirement.

Most important of all as a starting point is the actual short-term goal – the "immediate post-MBA" thing that Columbia is asking about. That's why we suggest starting with Columbia. Nail that answer down. Revise and refine it. Maybe even go through the EssaySnark App Accelerator on career goals if you want help in developing this essential element of your pitch. Get your ducks in a row in terms of what you want to do straight out of bschool. While you're at it, identify a clear vision for the longer-term future as well. Craft all that up into a compelling essay with a plan for your future career for the Columbia short-answer question.

Then, turn your attention to the NYU essay 1.

Doing Columbia's short-answer question first one is only so that you can carve out a direct answer to the career goals part, since they are forcing you to be so very precise in how you respond to that. Doing NYU's essay 1 next will help you based on the structured questions that they're asking.

To repeat: Just because the questions are best handled in a similar fashion, you still need to re-write your essays for one to the other. Don't be tempted to re-use one draft wholesale for the other school's app. There are enough nuances in what they're each asking – and the schools themselves are different enough – that you need to bring fresh thinking to both. But there are also some synergies you'll be able to take advantage of.

A Snarky Caveat

Do not re-use Columbia's career essay for Stern.
You need to do more with it.

We shouldn't have to explain this – you should know better than to assume that you can write one career essay and use it for multiple schools. Each one is asking their questions in a different way, and each school cares about different things.

There's a specific truth to recognize for NYU, however: **Stern only wants you if you really want them.** (This goes back to that discussion of yield we offered earlier.) Some other schools bank on their brand name and reputation and they presume that if they accept you, it's likely that you'll accept them. Not so with Stern. You need to show them you love them. One way to prove that is to write the Stern essays from scratch. That's the best way to avoid any unforced errors, like forgetting to change the word "Columbia" to "Stern" when you reuse an essay (yes, this happens all the time).

If there's any whiff in your essays or buried deep within your pitch to Stern that you are considering them in the runner-up position in your bschool application strategy, the Stern adcom will sniff it out. Cutting corners and reusing essays often results in a lackluster, uninspired pitch. If they feel you're calling it in with the essays you've submitted, then they could quite easily dismiss you and move on to the next Brave Supplicant in the stack.

Stern knows what Columbia is asking in their app. They can tell when an essay wasn't developed organically for them. They have no reason to give you the time of day if you are showing that kind of ambivalence towards them. And the best (worst?) way to show ambivalence is to do a sloppy job of converting an essay written for some other school and trying to pass it off as one you wrote for Stern.

Don't do that. Write your Stern essay fresh.

The NYU Essay Questions

Many top bschools redesign their application each season, to present new essay questions to each year's crop of candidates. Not Stern. Stern is consistent over time. The NYU essays haven't changed dramatically in years, and the things they've been looking for have been standard over a very long time.

In fact, Stern's Personal Expression was practically famous, having been featured on Marketplace, a public radio show, way back in 2005. Personal Expression was an innovative addition to the bschool application and it became a staple of the Stern essay questions. (Unfortunately the audio interview with Stern's admissions director Isser Gallogly has now been removed from the Marketplace site and we can't find an archive of it anywhere ☹.)

Stern was one of the first schools to explore other media and methods to invite applicants to present themselves in novel ways. This is proof of their interest in getting to know you, and their dedication to giving you, the applicant, a chance to show them who you really through your application assets.

What does this mean to you, Brave Supplicant?

First of all, because NYU's essays have been so standardized for so long, it means *they've seen it all before*. EssaySnark just took a gander back through some Stern essays submitted by a snapshot of our clients over the years, and man oh man do they sound alike. And are they ever boring. One reason schools mix up their essay questions each year is, we can only assume, because the adcom gets bored to tears reading essays written against the same prompt for so many admissions cycles in a row. (Another reason is that so many admissions consultants publish "Do it this way!" exhortations and those inevitably result in a crop of essays being submitted that all say the same things – that totally happened with Berkeley's "What song describes you?" question.)

But Stern has kept things constant. And that means that *it takes a lot to stand out from the pack.* In honest truth, that actually means it's *easy* to stand out from the pack, because the pack all sound alike. Look to the guidelines we're offering to you and you'll be presenting a Stern application that's sound, straightforward, and strong.

Remember that Stern is looking for good candidates; they need to admit a bunch of them every year. As one alum said to us once, "The atypical is typical at NYU." The Stern adcom will patiently review every item in your application packet to see if you are a candidate whom they should pursue. Even if you have goals that are very common, or you're coming from an oversubscribed candidate pool, they'll still take their time and read everything you submit. They won't cut corners and give your essays the once-over only because it sounds like a bunch of others'. Don't try to make your goals flamboyant and your essays stand out. The way to stand out is to answer the questions well and reveal yourself authentically in the essays.

Stern's consistent line of questioning over the years makes their job easier, since they have ridden this merry-go-round before. They know what they're looking for. When their essays are so similar for years on end, they can quickly spot the strong application when it wanders in the door.

What else does it mean? The fact that Stern kept its Personal Expression essay in place for so long – around ten years – means that it works for them. They're able to learn a lot about their applicants through this essay. This is especially true when applicants submit more than an "essay" – when you go beyond the 500-word piece and into some other medium to show them about yourself.

Because of this, EssaySnark suggests that you consider Option B for Stern Essay 2. We feel so strongly about this that we're going to codify it as a formal recommendation:

Snarky Strategy #5

A non-written Personal Expression essay can be a great way for you to directly share more of who you are with the Stern adcom.

We'll come back to the Personal Expression essay later, with some tips and tricks for how to go about crafting a good one. For now, we're just planting the seed in terms of what you should be thinking about with your Stern essay choices. You can do an essay for Personal Expression – or you can answer Option A instead, about your two paths – but in our experience, a well-executed non-written Personal Expression submission can really help.

Career Goals and Stern

As with many bschools, the career goals must form the foundation of your pitch to Stern. They are really, truly important. And the career goals are by far, with no competition, the main #1 place where Brave Supplicants fall down.

If you are a reapplicant and you didn't get into bschool last year, it's almost guaranteed to be because your career goals were a mess. And/or your profile was out of whack, like unrealistic GMAT score or flawed GPA, just like we've covered already. And even if those flaws were present, it's likely that the career goals kinda sucked too. It's that common of a problem.

So let's make sure you don't end up in that category, Brave Supplicant. Let's see what we can do to help coach you to some winning set of career goals for Stern.

Remember what we called out before, about the three categories that you need to cover? Let's review it again. The Stern adcom has labeled their questions in this way:

- Essay 1: Professional Aspirations
- Essay 2: Your Two Paths [or] Personal Expression

When you dig into the questions they want answered, they are asking you to tell them what you want to do (career goals) and why you need an MBA (why now/why Stern), what do you know about NYU (school fit), and more about yourself – either career-wise, or from a personal angle.

Sound like a lot? It's not. The Stern app is straightforward, and that's how you should be in addressing it. The first task is to define your goals.

EssaySnark's career goals exercise

This is an exercise that we used for years when starting a formal MBA admissions consulting engagement with a new client. This will serve you well as you begin to craft your answer to the NYU career goals question. It will actually serve you in tackling the goals question that any school asks, in any form or variety – that's why we include this section in many of these *SnarkStrategies Guides*. Once you map out your goals for the first school app, you'll be able to re-use them for the other schools, too.

Define Your Career Goals

Please complete this fill-in-the-blank exercise. This is a good first step for you to develop your ideas for career goals, in order to demonstrate to the adcom what you want to do and why an MBA is essential:

1. "After I get my MBA I will be/do X"

Add as much detail as you can – job title, industry or niche, functional area, specialty, example companies to work for, geography, etc.

[Write your answer here. Go ahead. Nobody will look at it.]

_____

_____

_____

_____

2. "My long term goal is to do Y"

Less detail needed, but must be clear and specific, and rational, given the s/t goal.

[Write this one down, too.]

_____

_____

_____

_____

3. "An MBA from NYU Stern is critical for me to achieve this because"

Solid reasons that point to the differentiation offered by NYU are critical here — you'll want to express how Stern will explicitly give you the skills you need for the short-term goal.

[This is important. Use more space if you need to.]

_____

_____

_____

_____

4. "Now is the right time for me to get an MBA because: "

A younger candidate would include a quick statement of why they feel they're ready, other candidates might describe how they need the MBA now to take advantage of the opportunities they see in their industry; all candidates should focus on career milestones, significant professional achievements, and other signs of "readiness" to show how you're at a point in your career where you will benefit from the MBA — this can be answered in a lot of different ways, so see what you can come up with on the "why now?" side.

[This is implicit in the NYU career goals question – it's embedded in the "at this point in your life?" bit.]

_____

_____

_____

_____

> The short-term goal should have significant detail, and the bschool experience needs to be the setup for that (bschool should be positioned as the best means possible to prepare you for that s/t goal). The long-term goal needs much less detail but it needs to be logical and achievable, given the interim goals. You wouldn't want to position bschool as prep for the l/t goal, only the short-term one.

Yes, even though NYU hasn't explicitly asked for a "title" in their essay question, it wouldn't hurt to put one in. That type of specificity can take you far. It shows that you've put some thought into it, that you've researched the options, that you know the industry. These sorts of details truly cannot hurt you, and in many ways, they will help you stand out.

You should spend some time on this. What most people come up with their first time out is far from sufficient. You may even need to go off and do some research on your target industry and find out what types of jobs are available and what you'd be doing in them. Do some digging. Flesh this out. An off-the-cuff set of career goals will not help you get into NYU.

So what's a bad career goal?

Let's look at a few examples.

> "I want to become a leader in the financial services industry."

We see this all the time. Sorry folks. "Leader" is meaningless. And, believe it or not, so is "financial services." Much too broad. Are you talking about a big bank? A hedge fund? A mutual fund or other investment management company? Even insurance companies are often lumped into "financial services." This sentence is near-meaningless. It doesn't tell us anything about *what you want to do*.

Here's another one:

> "I want to be on the executive team of a multinational corporation."

Same problem. Sure, "executive team" has a little more specificity than "leader" however it still doesn't tell us *what you want to do*. (Note the theme?) And "multinational corporation" is just a blob of a term. What type of corporation? In which country? If you're interested in some type of international angle to your career, then you need to say that! This term is communicating next to nothing — except to say that maybe you haven't really put that much thought into it yet.

The other issue with both of these "bad" examples (probably) is timing. It's unrealistic to assume you'll be much of a "leader" — at least, not on a grand scale or anything — within the timeframe that Stern is asking you to present with these career goals. Nobody can see the future. Nobody knows what you'll be doing in 15 years. And yet that's how long it would take for most people to gain the experience, skills, and connections to actually become a CFO or what have you. It's highly unlikely you'll be rocking that boat within the timeframe expected in a "short/long-term goals" question from any school. So, saying you'll be on the ELT of a big conglomerate is a little unrealistic, probably.

Instead, you need to focus on literally what type of job you'll get right when you come out of NYU, and then, carve out a plan for how you'll progress from there, to perhaps another position, and at most, one more, which you'll identify as your long-term target. That final job that you present as your long-term goal should be within a reasonable timeframe. The foreseeable future. Like, maybe ten years from now, max (even that is not really "foreseeable" given how quickly things change in our lives and the world these days).

Keep in mind that most people are promoted maybe once every two years. If you consider your long-term goal to be in the five- to eight-year post-MBA timeframe, that will help you see (hopefully) what might be a realistic target to present for the adcom. **Given where you're at today in your career (level/role/title/responsibilities), what is a probable trajectory for where you will end up in, say, the year 2022?**

If you need a little more space to capture your thinking on your long-term goal, go right ahead – and if you're entertaining multiple options, then this would be a good time to get those captured too.

_____

_____

_____

_____

One exception where it might fly to tell the adcom that you'll be "CEO"? If you're going to be working in a family business after you graduate. If that's the case, then it's fine to say you're going to be taking over the whole show. You have different challenges than most people in presenting your goals (which are outside the discussion of this guide) however this could work well in being realistic and believable.

What did we just say? Something about "realistic and believable"? Yes, that sounds good. This is something to make note of formally and officially. In fact, let's call it:

A Snarky Caveat

Your career goals must be *believable* and *achievable*.

We've alluded to this already, with the comments about timeframe and what's feasible to accomplish in the long-term goal horizon that the school expects. The NYU adcom is really, truly going to look at your goals and see if they make sense. Is this a plan that you will be able to pull off? Is it do-able? Or more like a pipe dream?

An important point for us to make here is: *Don't make stuff up*. The point of this exercise is not to present the most amazing, aggressive, flamboyant-sounding goals the school has ever seen. Actually, it's usually much more effective to present goals that are very standard, traditional, perhaps even a little run-of-the-mill.

Bschool candidates are always told that they have to stand out, that they have to differentiate themselves. Well guess what? The career goals essay is not the place to do this.

- **People are admitted to Stern because they have clear, rational, logical goals that the adcom can see will be achievable at their school.**

- **People are admitted to Stern because they are able to show how they are ready to pursue those goals, based on what they've done in the past.**

The best way to impress the Stern adcom is to show them that you've already built your career up to a certain point, and that you have a plan for where you want to take it from here, and you're looking for the advantage of a Stern MBA to do so. This means, you want to present career goals that MAKE SENSE, both given who YOU are, and given what Stern stands for and what they can offer to you.

If you've read the *SnarkStrategies Guide for Columbia Business School*, then you will recognize that this is similar advice to what EssaySnark provides there. But as we've been saying, *Columbia and Stern are very different*. You might be able to use the same career goals for both schools – and in fact you should, because you're the same person applying to both schools, so why the heck would your goals change simply because it's a different application? But you'll need to express your understanding of and appreciation for the respective schools' culture quite differently if you want to be successful at each.

It's pretty unusual that someone gets an offer from both Columbia and Stern unless they do their homework on each school individually and understand what they're about, and demonstrate that understanding within their presentation.

Bschools are not interchangeable, regardless of how similar their career goals essay questions may sound (or not). This is the essence of "school fit" – a term that gets bandied about in bschool admissions circles and which many people have no clue about. "School fit" is an expression of the school's culture, and the candidate's resonance with those qualities. It's a little subtle and perhaps somewhat esoteric, but it's very obvious when it's expressed appropriately in an application.

A few additional warnings:

- If you're looking to use bschool to make some **radical career change**, you have a bigger challenge. You need to show the adcom that you have transferable skills and are equipped to make the transition to the new field. This can be especially critical for those going in a dissimilar direction, e.g., IT guys wanting to go into finance. You'll need to show how you're ready to make this leap. This is a case where you might want to use Option A – Your Two Paths for Stern Essay 2, as a way to shore up your argument and help the adcom see that you've put a lot of thought into it.

- Conversely, if you're not showing ENOUGH transition — if your stated **short-term goal is too similar** (or even identical) to what you are already currently doing in your job today — then you're not giving the adcom enough evidence of why you need an MBA. You should position yourself as ADVANCING, and then show how the MBA is the one main requirement that you need to get from A to B.

A Snarky Caveat

The three most common mistakes with bschool career goals are:

- **They're too vague**

- **They're too ambitious**

- **They're too broad**

If your goals suffer from any of these sins, it's highly unlikely NYU Stern, or any top business school, will let you in.

- *Too vague* means saying you want to work in "financial services" or on an "executive team" or that you want to go into "international business." None of these are careers, they are concepts.

- *Too ambitious* is a goal that's written to impress the reader instead of being attainable for the candidate's actual skills and experience – often goals that involve starting a company/nonprofit/private equity fund fall into this category. It's fine to have an entrepreneurial goal, provided you lay the foundation appropriately for it.

- *Too broad* frequently happens when the applicant can't make up his mind and so he brings in multiple options of "I could do this or I might do that." While it could very well be true that you will pursue different options and paths once you're in the process of earning your MBA, it is usually a mistake to try and present all these different options to the adcom in the essays. There simply isn't room to provide an appropriate level of detail on more than one possible career path.

The Stern adcom tends to reward candidates who express confidence and conviction, who come in with an honest-to-goodness action plan. Sure, your life may take you in a different direction once the wheels are in motion. What the bschool folks want to see is that you're mature and responsible, that you know how to take control of your life and that you're able to make your own success. A well-crafted set of essays will communicate this.

In a nutshell: Keeping that **realistic and believable** guideline in mind as you refine your goals should help you avoid these problems.

One more note: Sometimes people actually make their career goals *too specific*. Usually EssaySnark is trying to cajole our clients in the opposite direction – typically their goals are not specific enough – however sometimes, we get a Brave Supplicant who takes this to an extreme. Case in point? One year we had a client state that her long-term goal was to be CMO (Chief Marketing Officer) of Apple.

Why is this a problem? Well, for starters, it implies that the Brave Supplicant thinks a little highly of herself, to assume that she's going to qualify for this cream-of-the-crop job. But the other issue: There's only one of these jobs in the whole wide world. Apple has just one CMO, and you can bet that there're a whole lotta people who'd love to be it.

A Snarky Caveat

We're serious about the *achievable* thing.
It's got to be achievable for YOU.

Sure, you very well may end up being Chief Marketing Officer at Apple in a decade or two – after all, the people who go to great schools like NYU often do end up in such high-visibility and high-impact roles. But you probably won't be there in the standard five to eight years post-MBA timeframe that the adcom has in mind when they ask about goals. What's worse, you're painting yourself into a bit of a box to say that this is the one and only job you aspire to. What if that one, very specific goal doesn't pan out? It's actually too narrowly focused, to define a long-term goal so precisely. It is unrealistic.

Instead, broaden your goal out, either by position ("a senior-level position in marketing") and/or by company ("at a leading company such as Apple or ..."). Be sure to name more than one company. Everyone wants to go to work at Apple and Google and Goldman.

If you have a 3.89 GPA and a 750 GMAT and an amazing early career progression thus far, then maybe it will be believable to name the uppermost crust of companies. But if you're more middle-of-the-road in terms of how your profile presents, be conscious of how this comes across. Is it really believable that you're going to take your Chevrolet to Buckingham Palace? Don't you think maybe they're only looking for Rolls-Royces? If yours is a good but middling profile, and you name a second-tier company as a viable target for your future career path, it'll help you look a little less fond of yourself. It'll reinforce your humility and self-awareness.

Self-confidence is good; self-cockiness is not. By listing out some options of appropriate and achievable companies you'd be targeting for your career, you'll help the reader see what you think of yourself. Remember that whole EQ thing that Stern cares about? This will take you far in helping the adcom be comfortable that you're both humble, and realistic, and perhaps the kind of person that they'd like to welcome on campus.

Essay 1: Professional Aspirations

Now that you have your short-term goal clearly defined, are you ready to start writing? Nope, not yet. The next step in drafting your Stern Essay 1 is to look at your complete Stern essay strategy.

You should start your planning process with Stern Essay 1 by first deciding how you will approach Stern Essay 2.

Why? Because you need to know upfront if you have to cover absolutely everything about goals and why Stern in this one 750-word essay, or if you have a 750-word essay and a 500-word essay to communicate the full story.

Stern Essay 1 Strategy: Identify which option for Essay 2

We've already stated that many applicants will do themselves a favor by choosing to tackle the Personal Expression option – and, with that, by doing a non-written essay, such as an audio or video submission, or something visual like a PowerPoint slideshow. At this stage of your essay development process, you don't have to know what you'd present in such a non-written essay, but you should figure out pretty quickly whether or not you're going to go that route, or if you're going to use Option A for Stern Essay 2 instead.

If you legitimately have thought of multiple possible paths that you're interested in exploring for your future career, then Option A might be a good choice. We're not convinced that this is a great strategy for most people, however. Often when we see people with multiple ideas about their future, it only serves to undermine the idea that they even know why they want an MBA in the first place. After all, your career goals are your pitch – they are the way that you convince the adcom that you need an MBA, based on a specific future path you're going to pursue. If you have too many ideas floating around in your head about what you want to do in the future, then to us, that just means you need to do more work to figure things out first.

We even have heard some admissions consultants advise that the two paths you present in an Option A essay *should* be very different – like strategy consulting, or working in a charter school. When we saw that, we were like, "Huh?" The way you'd prepare for, and execute on, those two different careers is so radically different that they're almost in their own universes. Presenting two completely unique goals like that could easily raise many more questions for the adcom than it satisfies. We haven't seen anyone with such divergent goals pull off a convincing argument for how and why they fit together.

Remember, bschool is tremendously fast-paced, even frantic. You have opportunities raining down on you constantly, which is great – but if, coming in to the experience, you don't know what you want to do after you graduate, then how will you choose which opportunities to focus on? Everyone says that bschool flies by super fast. If you're not focused and clear on what you're targeting, you could get lost in the whirlwind and lose out. Stern's admissions director said that "business school is the place to get it done, not to figure it out."

For these reasons, we don't recommend presenting two paths in Essay 2 Option A that are radically opposed from one another.

And, based on the advantages that it can afford to you, we recommend that Essay 2 Option B is a better one for most people to choose. A good Personal Expression essay will, in almost every case, communicate more about you to the adcom than the hypothetical cases you would present in a Two Paths essay.

Remember of course that it's your application strategy. We're not trying to dictate which direction to go in... but as you now have gathered, we do feel pretty strongly that the Personal Expression option can do more good for many Brave Supplicants than submitting another essay would.

Please don't feel pressured though. If you feel that you have plenty to say about the Two Paths question, then you should absolutely use that for your Stern strategy. You just need to make your choice now, before you start planning the contents of Stern Essay 1, or you may end up having to do some juggling and make some sacrifices or less-optimal decisions in trying to get your material allocated well among the two different essays you're giving to work with.

If you choose to do Option A in Essay 2 then you could use some of that essay real estate to go into more details on why you want to go to Stern. If you choose the Personal Expression option for Essay 2, then you probably need to cover the bulk of your "why Stern" answer here, in Essay 1.

So, you might want to map out your strategy for Essay 2 before going too far with identifying material for Essay 1.

Pitching an entrepreneurial goal to NYU

We're going to detour for a second now, since this is very important.

We mentioned earlier that NYU has some incredible resources and a supportive community for entrepreneurs on campus, and we strongly believe that it's one of the best places to launch or build a business. It's an expensive way to do it, but you would have an excellent support system around you. Companies like Twitter and Foursquare have connections to NYU and you'll see lots of exciting speakers on campus all the time, along with the standard business plan/VC competitions etc.

The problem is, how do you position your goals in your Stern essays if you want to be an entrepreneur?

This is where lots of BSers fall down.

If you already have a company started, then you're ahead of the curve. What you'll want to do is present some specifics of how far along you are, do you have employees, what's your revenue, and particularly why do you feel that it's important to go to Stern and get an MBA as your next step.

It's trickier if you have not a business but an idea. This can be a hard sell – not just to Stern, but to any admissions team.

This is where the Stern Essay 2 Option A comes in.

If you do not yet have your business off the ground, and you really truly plan on using bschool to start one, then you'll probably want to use the Two Paths essay to expand on your thinking.

Or, you might present your current ideas around when you'll do this new venture that you have in mind. Maybe you are looking to pursue a more traditional immediate post-MBA job, possibly in a new sector or to gain relevant experiences that will be needed for your future venture, and then sometime down the road after graduation is when you intend to do this entrepreneurship thing.

What NYU cares about is THE PLAN.

You need to have it all mapped out.

What EssaySnark frequently sees is pipe dreams. Or ideas with holes big enough to drive a convoy of Mack trucks through.

Pitching an entrepreneurial goal is more difficult (in some ways) than a traditional set of goals. You need to account for these different angles. If you come in with the strength of your convictions, you can easily impress the adcom – but too many times, we see people flounder with their apps due to half-baked goals and unrealistic ideas. Think things through, Brave Supplicant.

How to structure Stern Essay 1

Now that the pieces are coming together for your overall essay strategy, it's time to look at the required elements for Essay 1. Let's ask Stern admissions how to do it – they spell things out pretty clearly:

> *Essay 1 - Professional Aspirations*
>
> - *Why pursue an MBA (or dual degree) at this point in your life?*
>
> - *What actions have you taken to determine that Stern is the best fit for your MBA experience?*
>
> - *What do you see yourself doing professionally upon graduation?*

The Stern adcom asks their goals question differently than almost any other school does – with the exception, this year, of Columbia, which has a similar angle. NYU asks you to speak to your goals from "this point in your life", while Columbia's question starts off with "given your individual background." In both cases, it helps tremendously if you give the adcom a snapshot of the elements of your career, and/or your life, that are specifically relevant to your intended future goals. Many bschools don't ask anything about the past in their career goals question. Stern wants to know why you're capable and qualified to pursue this great thing you're laying out for yourself, based on who you are today, and why is now the right time.

Another big component to the Stern essay is, they want to see how you approach the question itself. They want to make sure you can read and follow directions. They care about how you break down the problem of developing your essay, and how you construct your thoughts in response to the questions they've asked. What you say definitely matters, and how you say it is also very important.

Besides laying out literally what your goals are, this particular essay question lets you also explain why you're ready to pursue those goals. The most effective way to do that is to give some specific example that summarizes or highlights the strengths of your career and communicates more than can be seen with a quick glance at your resume. You might want to showcase the wins, the turning points, or the major successes. Perhaps you could mention some big achievements and where they brought you. Drill down into a few those key moments, using them to answer the question about your "professional experiences" and illustrate to the reader how you're prepared for this next step.

The "this point of your life" question is asking for highlights or brief call-outs to the most critical elements or experiences that provide the platform from which you will be pursuing your goals. In other words, why is now the time for the MBA? Why are you ready to go do this new thing you want to do? This can come through in a gazillion ways, but it should definitely be addressed upfront in the essay.

In terms of the goals themselves: These should be a natural outgrowth of what you've done to date. It should be fairly obvious why you want to go do this new thing, based on how you present it, and your background. It shouldn't be such a radical departure from everything you've done before that we are skeptical in seeing how you'll pull it off. You can present a big career jump in the essays – you can tell the adcom how you want to go do something quite different from what you've done before – but you need to establish some continuity in terms of how you're prepared for the challenges you'll face. The best essays show how you have had a plan and you have been executing on it. You don't want to come across as an accidental traveler. The elements of your past must fit together into where you say you want to go in the future. This messaging and fitting-together of the elements is up to you. Just don't toss out something so unrelated to your past that it makes no sense for how you'll get there. The adcom wants to see what your thinking was in choosing the path that you have.

Wow, EssaySnark said a lot about the career goals. They're important – but so is everything else about this essay. The second question to Essay 1 is where you impart your love for Stern. This is where you pull out all the stops and talk with enthusiasm about what you know about Stern, and why those attributes are important to you. This is where:

- You impress the adcom with all the efforts you've made to research the program, reach out to the students and alumni, interact with the admissions team, and engage with the Stern community

- You articulate your understanding for what Stern's about in a way that shows how you will leverage same in your own educational process

This essay should talk about *specifics*. With this question, the Stern adcom is encouraging you to come to campus, or to meet the admissions team as they travel the world. Do some networking, ask some questions. Take the time to find out if Stern is really the right place for you, and then reflect on the reasons why – and put THAT in this essay.

A Snarky Caveat

If you visited campus or attended an info session – *tell them about it!* Include the month of your interaction in Essay 1 (include the year, too, if it was not recent). Name some names.

The way to make a strong pitch to Stern or any school is to include specifics in your arguments. Nowhere is this more important than in answer to the second part of Stern Essay 1.

Next up for advice on how to map out your Stern goals essay is how to allocate your 750 words.

Snarky Strategy #6

Essay 1 has three questions in it.
Devote equal space to all three.

Remember that this is ONE ESSAY. It's up to 750 words total (it's fine to go over that somewhat, just don't be extreme), written in a cohesive, single draft with each question answered, and the answers constructed together in a way that they flow from one to the next. In other words, it's not three separate essays, nor is it three separate sections with subheadings or titles dividing it up. One essay, covering three topics.

You don't have to literally plan for 250 words for each of the sub-questions they're asking. If we were forced to prioritize, we'd say that the goals are the most important – provided that you're conveying your background sufficiently well in your resume and through your recommendations. Remember that the essays are just one part of your app. The adcom will have access to everything else, too – your work history form that you upload, the transcripts from your schools, all of that. What you say about your goals is your justification for why you need the MBA in the first place. If you need to use more of Essay 1 for that topic, go ahead. You can afford to squeeze down the space allotted to the first part – why is now the right time – as long as you're conveying your background and strengths sufficiently through your other application assets.

You will undoubtedly run out of room with this essay. We're glad that Stern has maintained the 750-word length limit for this, in the face of word limit reductions from so many other schools. Starting with outlines to sketch out your ideas and plan your approach is a good strategy (our Essay Ideas App Accelerator can show you how).

You also need to give some thought as to what order you'll arrange things in. There are no set-in-stone rules for how to structure this essay, though you should stick to a generally chronological presentation, which is how they've asked the question. The first chunk should be covering the past (why now is the right time to go for an MBA), the next chunk should talk about the present (what have you done to learn about Stern and why are you convinced they're the school for you) and then the last chunk should take the reader through the future (what do you want to do with the MBA). You could answer the three questions in a different order, but if you do, make sure to give clear signals to your reader in terms of what you're talking about where, with good transitions between the topics.

And remember that the second question, about how you've learned about Stern, is just as important as the others. Remember what we said at the very beginning of this *Guide*, with SnarkStrategy #1 and community? This is where you can reveal some of what you've learned, and value, about Stern.

Similarly, don't shortchange your answer to the first question about why you want an MBA and why you want one now. Many Brave Supplicants breeze past this with an unsatisfactory sentence or two, and that is a mistake.

How should you literally start the essay?

At risk of completely contradicting what we just advised in terms of writing your essay in chronological order, we want to offer a tip that we feel makes many career goals essays flow best:

EssaySnark recommends presenting a direct statement of your career goals in the opening sentence. This is often an effective way to start things off with Essay 1.

You can use the response to Columbia's short-answer question that you developed as your first step in tackling your essays. Start your Stern essay with the thing you intend to do immediately after bschool.

Beginning with this information – which is the crux of the whole essay and the answer to the third question they've asked – can give the reader context for the entire essay. You can state your goal(s) and then move back to a discussion of "why now" - you needn't include a full paragraph at the goals at the very beginning. By including the minimum goals statement there, you're giving context and a frame to the reader, to better understand everything else that you are presenting in answer to their questions.

The one risk with this is that the essay could appear to have been written for another school. If you can reuse some of the language in the Stern essay prompt in that first sentence, or in some other way key off of a Stern-specific element in your opening, it will help to show that yes, this was crafted for Stern.

Hopefully we haven't confused you unnecessarily. The most important thing is, answer each of the three questions within your Stern Essay 1, and be clear on the goals themselves. How you slice and dice and order and present the information is largely up to you. If it's logical, and fits together, and flows, then you're good to go.

In terms of flow:

A Snarky Caveat

> Don't divide up your Stern career essay into three separate sections.
> Don't use headings. Make it an integrated presentation, start to finish.

They've structured the essay prompt with the three individual questions in order to guide you in how to structure your response, however you should *not* write separate answers to the separate sections. Your essay should be smooth, and complete, with a formal introduction, fluid transitions between each major idea or section, and a conclusion that wraps everything up at the end.

The conclusion is important. Please don't omit the conclusion. This is a long essay, you have room to write a formal ending that ties your points together and ends on a strong note.

In terms of length: Because this is a longer essay, you should be able to convey what you need within the limit provided by the adcom. You can go over 750 words – they don't count words in your submitted essays – but you shouldn't go bonkers with it. A 775-word essay is fine; anything over 800 words, probably not.

Stern Essay 1 is a critically important part of your application. Plan for significant time to map out your strategy, and even more time to rewrite your draft. Don't rush this one. Good writing requires effort and that effort takes time. Be prepared for a full process of revision and rework to make your essay shine.

Essay 2 Option A: Your Two Paths

We've already given some possible drawbacks to choosing this essay option, and some situations where it's a good idea. If you decide to go with Option A on Stern Essay 2, then here's some guidelines to keep in mind as you develop your ideas:

1. This essay needs to convey new information about you. Look at what you're presenting already in Essay 1, in the resume, and in your recommendations, and see what's missing. Option A could be a way to give the adcom another side of yourself that you're unable to present elsewhere. If you do, be sure to use concrete examples and hard facts when you tell them about this other element to your profile.

2. This essay also needs to showcase your interest in Stern. To some degree, this essay is an extension of Essay 1; the same rules and guidelines apply here. Your job is to add color to the plans you've laid out in the main career goals essay, and to give the adcom new insights about your future – and about why you want to go to Stern. Use every opportunity to weave in angles from your research into NYU and showcase why you feel that it's the best place for you to study for your MBA.

3. Even with that, keep the focus on yourself, and on tangibles. It's often tempting to go off on a discussion about industry trends and market forces in this type of essay, as an attempt to impress the reader with all that you know about your intended future career. A tiny bit of that is fine, but too much of it is taking away from the main purpose, which is to share more of yourself with the adcom. Review everything you plan to include in this essay through the filter of, "What does it tell the reader about ME?" If you have too much discussion of non-essentials, they will detract from your pitch for admission to the Stern MBA.

This needs to be an essay of substance, not one of ideas. Don't wax poetic about possibilities and dreams. Keep your plans anchored to earth. Give good reasons for why you'd pursue one path versus another – and be sure to incorporate your interest in Stern as part of that.

Remember the warnings we issued earlier, about the two different paths you present. If you're giving the adcom a pair of future goals that are so radically divergent from each other, it could actually discredit your claim that you're ready for bschool. Step back and look at the messages you're sending by submitting the two alternate paths. A smart individual in today's world will keep options open and stay flexible. An ill-equipped individual will forge ahead without regard to reality, and likely will get nowhere. Don't make the adcom wonder if you're chasing windmills. Keep your plans reasonable. Cross-check them against each other. What you present must be rational and sensible, and internally consistent.

In terms of your final product: There is no reason why this essay should run long. As with most essays, you can go over the 500-word limit, but in this case you should not do so to any extreme. We strongly suggest keeping the final draft for Option A under 525 words total.

And don't forget the formalities of an introduction and a conclusion. Just like Essay 1, this needs to be a professionally-written essay that answers the questions they've asked, and does so cleanly, with an easy-to-digest structure and an argument that flows.

Essay 2 Option B: Personal Expression

Finally we come to it: The famous Personal Expression essay. Yes we have a bias; we believe that this is your chance to shine.

If all you have to offer is another written essay, you should not feel ashamed to do that. (Poetry also works.)

Just be sure to directly answer the question, and provide new information to the adcom that is relevant to the domain they've asked in. A couple paragraphs of specific, concrete, vivid examples about who you are or where you've come from or what you're interested in can be completely appropriate for this essay. This is where any of your hidden hobbies may prove useful. Just make sure it's bschool-relevant, and that you don't stray into TMI territory (check out the EssaySnark blahg for some posts on sharing "too much information" in your essays).

At the same time: Many people do more than "just an essay" for Stern. It's one of the few schools that actively encourages candidates to "think outside the box" (pardon the cliché). If you have any artistic abilities whatsoever, this is a great place to let them come out.

And if you do not? *Don't sweat it.* This is not the time to take up oilpainting if you've never done it before. And you should also be strategic. Yes, if you are your family's best knitter and you have knitted sweaters for everyone at the holidays for the past five years running, sure, you might consider knitting a sweater as your Personal Expression. But is that the very best way to present yourself? Knitting is somewhat unusual, it's a little quirky, it's charming. It could be a nice aspect of your life to share with the school. But is it *all* that you'd want to share? Your Personal Expression submission has specific size restrictions. You probably wouldn't want to send along a knitted sweater, PLUS a poem you wrote, PLUS a photocollage depicting your ideal career path... You'd need to choose among them.

EssaySnark is not trying to put the kibosh on any one of these ideas. Any of them could absolutely work for you. Our main point is here that *your "essay" needs to have a point.* Sometimes we hear about interesting ideas that Brave Supplicants come up with for Personal Expression, but they are only "interesting" and we have trouble seeing what "the point" is.

In other words: Step back and ask yourself, what are you communicating with this submission? What is your takeaway message meant to be? What impression are you trying to send?

Not all Personal Expression ideas are created equal. Some are spot-on relevant and appropriate, and they convey so much about the candidate. Some leave us scratching our heads and wondering what the purpose is.

A Snarky Caveat

> **The most important consideration with the Personal Expression essay is that you are communicating *to your Stern classmates.* Whatever you construct and deliver should be geared towards your future peers – not to the adcom.**

Our best advice for this essay? Design and present your content from the perspective as if you're trying to make a friend. This is especially true if you submit a written essay. Don't write to impress. While the tone should still be formal and professional, beware of sounding too stiff – and definitely try to avoid sounding like you're trying to "wow" someone with fancy language and expensive-sounding words.

A very rough guideline is to treat this as if you were talking to someone you just met in a bar – someone you just found out is a Sternie. What would you want that person to know about you? What would you tell them? How would you present yourself in a way that shows your enthusiasm for Stern while also highlighting something cool or unique or fun or exciting about your own fabulous self (and in a way that doesn't make it seem like you think that you're *too* fabulous)???

This is where the EQ part plays in. You want to share with them what's appropriate in the context of a bschool app (nitty-gritty details of your personal life probably don't need to be shared), that gives the adcom a taste of who you are and what makes you tick, that helps you stand out from the crowd (in only positive ways!), that shows how you'd fit into the Stern community and add to the experience of your peers.

A Snarky Caveat

It's OK to use a video or PowerPoint created for another school as your Stern Personal Expression – but make it personal to Stern!

MIT has an optional video component to their app, and for many years, Chicago Booth has had a 4-slide PowerPoint essay requirement as part of theirs. You can potentially leverage the work you've done for one of those schools with your Stern Personal Expression – as long as you're careful, and attentive, and you modify it appropriately.

If you submit a 4-slide PowerPoint PDF for Stern, then Stern will obviously assume you're also applying to Chicago Booth. And they'll also assume that they're not important enough to you to do more work than the minimum. This isn't the best message to be sending. The schools know you're applying to multiple places... but you'd better make sure there's no trace of Booth left anywhere in that PPT when you upload it to NYU. Even better: Make it five slides, or three.

Lots and lots of people reuse audio or video created for different schools. They create one photograph-laden PowerPoint presentation and then they multitask it for use in these other applications. No problem with that, but don't assume that the same messaging you create for a pitch to one school will automatically be the best messaging for Stern. At a minimum, you'll probably want to customize it further for NYU. And the adcom at NYU will know that you're repurposing content.

Even so, EssaySnark thinks that a photo-essay (PPT) is usually better than a written essay for the Stern Personal Expression, since it's generally more "personal" – the adcom will at least get to see what you look like. And, most people can hack their way around a PowerPoint. It doesn't have to be a professionally-rendered presentation, it just has to be clean, well-organized, and easy to understand.

If you're up for the challenge, we invite you to go one step further for Personal Expression. Creating a video of yourself is one of the best ways to showcase the "real you" to Stern – or at least, a "more real you" than most people can convey in their writing.

We know of several Sternies who, we are convinced, made it into NYU on the strength of their Personal Expression videos alone. These are people who had some significant weaknesses on their profiles, who in some cases weren't the best writers (which showed on the essays), who had standard goals and were otherwise rather non-descript. Yet they each created powerhouse videos that wowed us – each in their own way.

There's no formula for what makes a good video presentation to a school. And, we're reluctant to share too many specifics on what others have done before, because we worry that it will quash your own natural ideas from coming forth. You should never copy what someone else has done – particularly anything gimmicky. The adcoms remember the videos they see, and they will instantly know if you borrowed too liberally from someone else's. Don't be a copycat. Make something that's uniquely your own. Don't worry about whether or not the video looks completely polished. You do NOT need a professional-quality production for your Stern video – and in fact, if it's too overdone, then it sort of defeats the purpose in showing the adcom about you. Don't pay for someone to produce your video for you. Make it yourself, or maybe with the help of a friend or too. But unless you're going into the Tisch program, then it hardly makes sense to create an MBA admissions video that's Oscar-quality.

Let the real you shine through. Be authentic, and honest. Share parts of yourself that you otherwise could not in any other way. Be personal. Show a humorous side, if you're so inclined. Don't make it over-rehearsed or phony.

The best test for a bschool admissions video is, is it you who comes across on the screen? If so, you're golden.

EssaySnark will be developing a specific how-to guide on creating bschool admissions videos – look for it in the EssaySnark Bookstore.

Some Dos and Don'ts for Stern Personal Expression

These are not rules per se, but they are some guidelines that we think are appropriate to offer up, given how many really bad Essay 3s we've seen over the years. These mostly apply to PowerPoint presentations since those are by far the most common.

1. If you write an essay, don't make it any longer than 500 words – and shorter is probably better.

2. If you use photos, such as in a PowerPoint presentation, consider including captions to help the reader understand what she's seeing – but those should be short! Concise! Brief! Just a few words or a phrase, not full paragraphs.

3. In fact, if you have not written a formal essay, then there should be very little text overall in your presentation. If you've got a PowerPoint presentation with photos and graphics, then avoid having huge blocks of text alongside.

4. If you do have any text in the PowerPoint slides, keep the font size relatively large

5. A chronological presentation is typically best: Start with slide 1 on old stuff and move to present day on the last one.

6. There should be a connection between the slides; don't slap together three or four completely unrelated segments within a single PPT

7. Stock photographs are lame (this is just EssaySnark's opinion). If you're going to use photos, make them of YOU.

8. It can look messy if you combine photos with clipart. Try to stick to one theme. (In general, most clipart looks pretty cheesy, but again, that's just our opinion. If you do use it, then stick with one style.)

9. Be very careful with colors and fonts. Too many of either and you risk looking frazzled.

EssaySnark will never offer ideas or suggestions for Stern Personal Expression. If we did, then everyone would be sending in submissions that were all the same. However, we are happy to comment on the ideas that you come up with. If you want to run your Personal Expression plans past us, to see what we think, we can offer a thumbs-up or thumbs-down judgment on it. Send it along to gethelpnow@essaysnark.com and we'll let you know our reaction.

A note about sending a physical Personal Expression essay

Stern says your submission must be "postmarked" by the due date. That's the date stamp that the post office puts on the package (or, the date that a commercial carrier accepted it for shipment). The rationale: in the U.S., this "postmarked by" date is the method used to determine if our taxes are deemed "filed" by the IRS – if they are mailed (postmarked) on the day they are due, then you've submitted on time and no penalties would be assessed.

Typically anything mailed from one of the 50 states will arrive at its U.S. destination within two or three business days, so if you're mailing from the U.S., and it's postmarked on the deadline, the Stern adcom will have it that week. Thus this "postmarked by" date is guaranteed to get the item to them in a reasonable window – and, it eliminates the frantic calls from gazillions of Brave Supplicants to the admissions office asking for confirmation that their essay was received on time. If you know you have it postmarked on or before the due date, then you know you met their requirement.

But if you're mailing from overseas, you should get it out sooner!! And, use FedEx or a similar service for expedited delivery. Standard surface mail from some countries takes FOREVER. The adcom won't be able to start processing your application until all components are received. Don't jeopardize your app because your Personal Expression submission is on a slow boat.

No matter where you are mailing from, use tracking on a package or letter being sent to any adcom, so that you know when it gets there – the stress of not knowing what happened to something this important is just not worth it! (The adcoms typically cannot tell you when or if something has arrived, they get too much volume to respond to individual requests.)

What to Do Next

We've already told you about how helpful it would be to visit NYU. We'll say it again, in case you didn't believe us the first time. GO VISIT NYU. Check out the campus. Meet some people. Explore the city of New York. You should also do additional firsthand research, like checking out the professors, learning which amazing people in the world are alumni, reading up on them. And of course, you need to work on those essays.

EssaySnark reviews essays for the top business schools on our blahg (for free!) at http://essaysnark.com. We've got lots of material in articles and Q&A about Stern there. If you have questions we can help with about Stern or any of your other applications, feel free to email us at gethelpnow@essaysnark.com or find us on Twitter (@EssaySnark).

Look for other *SnarkStrategies Guides* (digital and paperback) at your favorite bookseller or on the EssaySnark blahg.

"Over time, advanced economies will need to invest in human capital, skills and social safety nets to increase productivity and enable workers to compete, be flexible and thrive in a globalized economy."

NOURIEL ROUBINI

www.ingramcontent.com/pod-product-compliance
Lightning Source LLC
Chambersburg PA
CBHW080527110426
42742CB00017B/3259